Death Drop

Death Drop

Melanie Jackson

Orca currents

ORCA BOOK PUBLISHERS

Library and Archives Canada Cataloguing in Publication

Jackson, Melanie, 1956-, author
Death drop / Melanie Jackson.
(Orca currents)

Issued in print and electronic formats.
ISBN 978-1-4598-1192-8 (paperback).—ISBN 978-1-4598-1193-5 (pdf).—
ISBN 978-1-4598-1194-2 (epub)

I. Title. II. Series: Orca currents
PS8569.A265D43 2016   jC813'.6   C2016-900779-0
C2016-900780-4

First published in the United States, 2016
Library of Congress Control Number: 2016931884

Summary: In this high-interest novel for middle readers, Zeke gets caught up in a
mystery involving a missing child, a thrill ride and a priceless piece of art.

*Orca Book Publishers is dedicated to preserving the environment and has
printed this book on Forest Stewardship Council® certified paper.*

Orca Book Publishers gratefully acknowledges the support for its
publishing programs provided by the following agencies: the Government
of Canada through the Canada Book Fund and the Canada Council
for the Arts,and the Province of British Columbia through
the BC Arts Council and the Book Publishing Tax Credit.

Cover photography by Getty Images
Author photo by Bart Jackson

ORCA BOOK PUBLISHERS
www.orcabook.com

Printed and bound in Canada.

19 18 17 16 • 4 3 2 1

"But you knew there would always be the spring"

—Ernest Hemingway,
A Moveable Feast

Chapter One

"She's gone."

It was a little girl with an English accent. She sounded cross. She was nothing to do with me. I thought she was talking to someone else in line.

I kept staring up at Death Drop from my place in the line on the sidewalk.

At 170 feet high, attached to a black tower, the elevator was Vancouver's newest thrill ride. Death Drop plunged its passengers down at forty miles an hour. Fifteen times the speed of a normal elevator. Faster than gravity.

Like the tower, the elevator was black—with one difference. It had a huge blood-red pomegranate painted on one side.

Death Drop was based on a Greek myth. Hades, the king of the under-world, gave a pomegranate to a beautiful woman named Persephone, whom he had kidnapped. She ate a few seeds. Who wouldn't? Pomegranates are bittersweet, refreshing.

But sly Hades had put a spell on the pomegranate. Eating the seeds meant that Persephone had to marry Hades and spend half of every year with him.

Behind Death Drop, people kayaked on False Creek. The water was blue-green in the sun. The kayakers didn't seem to be thinking about nature though.

With their paddles, they pointed up to the tower that had been built for the elevator. Everybody was talking about the big drop.

To reach the elevator, you walked up the tower's curving, windowless corridors. You got treated to special horror effects—*To die for!* the ads promised. There was even a famous painting of Persephone, on loan from England.

I had arrived early for baseball practice at the park across the street. I'd decided to see what all the hype was about.

In orange, flame-shaped letters, a sign explained that groups of twenty at a time went in. The next group had to wait until the first group crashed down in the elevator.

While waiting, I tossed my baseball up and down.

"She's gone."

I looked down. A kid with sausage-like blond curls was talking to me.

Out of the whole Death Drop lineup, why come to me for help? I didn't look very respectable. My LA Angels T-shirt was streaked with mud.

Besides, I was a boy. Kids with problems needed a nice lady. A middle-aged, motherly type.

"You can't find your mom?" I asked. I didn't put a lot of friendliness into my voice.

She scowled. "My *aunt*," she said as if I should know.

"Right," I said. I glanced up and down the line of people. If I left it to help the kid, I'd lose my place.

I spotted an attendant at the entrance. He wore black jeans and a black T with a pomegranate design. He was pale, with a pinched expression like he didn't want to be there. Maybe he thought he was too good to be taking tickets.

I told the kid, "That's who you need. Someone who works here."

She shook her head. The sausage-like curls bounced. She pointed to me. To my baseball shirt.

"Angels," she said. "Angels help people."

Screams ripped through the air. Death Drop was plunging!

The top half of the elevator slid back. Now the passengers could see the ground hurtling toward them. The elevator tipped forward. They screamed louder.

Then—flames leaped from the earth. Death Drop zoomed right into them.

Or so it appeared. The flames were gas-powered, from jets built in a circle around the elevator. No one was at risk of getting burned.

The elevator landed. People staggered out. One guy, looking kind of green, ran into a washroom.

The blond kid was still watching me.

With a great effort, I kept my voice patient. "About my T-shirt. The Los

Angeles Angels are a team. See, I'm into baseball. I'm a pitcher."

The girl nodded. "You will help me."

I was not getting through to this kid. I wasn't used to dealing with children. I had no younger siblings. And my life consisted of baseball, baseball, baseball.

I decided the best plan was to forge ahead. I smiled brightly at her. "So! Now that we've cleared that up, why don't you go over to that guy in black. He'll—"

Take care of you, I meant to say. I never got the words out.

The kid opened her mouth wide and howled. Tears sprang from her eyes. I'd never seen anything like it.

People turned to stare. They looked from me to the kid and back again. The stares turned to glares. I was being mean. I was bullying a little kid.

I gave up. I took the girl's hand. "Let's go find your aunt."

She kept bawling. But she let me lead her to the attendant.

"I have a lost child," I began.

The attendant was telling a boy with thick glasses that he didn't meet the height requirement. He pointed to a cardboard cutout of a grinning red demon with horns and a tail. A sign underneath warned, *If you're shorter than the demon, you're too young to ride Death Drop!*

I recognized the boy. Dieter Crane. The Deet, we called him. He was the class bookworm.

He was also a pest about baseball. Dieter showed up to every practice, begging Coach to let him on the team. But brainy Deet had skipped ahead two years in school, so he was younger than the rest of us. He was too young for the team, Coach said.

Every practice, Coach roared at him to scram. But it didn't put Dieter off.

He wasn't put off now either. He scrunched up his nose under his glasses and argued with the attendant. He said age shouldn't be a factor.

I tried again. "I have a lost—"

Without looking, the attendant snapped, "Lost-and-found is inside."

Like the blond kid was a misplaced flip-flop or sunhat.

I began to feel sorry for Blondie. Annoying or not, she deserved better.

I led her inside. Behind us, the Deet was insisting, "But I'm mature for my age!"

We were in a dark passageway. Above us, a red puppet demon jeered at us. "The higher they climb, the harder they fall!" He cackled with laughter.

Someone slammed into me.

"Sorry," Dieter exclaimed. He squinted up at me. "Zeke Sheldon! Hi, Zeke!"

The attendant shouted, "Come back here, Four Eyes!"

Pushing past other visitors, the Deet zoomed around the first curve.

The attendant marched to a door I hadn't noticed. A gleaming green-neon sign on it said *Office. Private.*

"Let's try in there," I suggested to Blondie. "Maybe your aunt's waiting for you."

I pushed the door open into a bright, sunlit office.

The attendant was at the desk. He was whining into a phone. His voice had a nasal quality, like it was designed for complaining. "You're the manager. Come on, give me backup. I can't deal with hooligans."

I didn't think of Dieter as a hooligan. He was just determined.

I noticed the attendant's name on a badge, in flame letters: *Smythe Sadler,*

Assistant Manager. He wasn't much older than I was.

I said, "Hey, Smythe, I have a lost little girl here. I'm betting her aunt is worried."

Smythe slammed the phone down. He swooped between Blondie and me.

He said, "I'll get the manager on this. She'll take care of it."

Blondie rolled her eyes. She heaved a big sigh and sat down. She swung her feet hard and high at Smythe. He had to dodge to avoid being kicked.

"Uh…" I felt bad leaving Blondie here. I didn't like her being referred to as *it*.

The attendant ran his tongue over his teeth. "We will deal with this. *Go*."

I went back out to the passageway. The demon puppet was jeering again. I thought about Smythe having to listen to that all day. No wonder he looked so sour.

I wasn't sure what to do. Line up again? Baseball practice was starting soon. Coach didn't tolerate lateness.

I had a lot riding on Coach's good opinion of me. He had pull with a couple of universities that offered base-ball scholarships.

As I stepped out into the sunshine, I thought maybe I should just go over to the park and wait for the rest of the team.

I noticed a girl with dark-red hair beside the entrance. She gave me a green-eyed glance, then went back to scribbling on her pad.

Smythe swept out of the building. He was scowling and licking his teeth some more. A nervous tic. I wondered if he wore down enamel doing that.

"Why aren't you at work?" he snapped at the girl.

"Sorry, Smythe. I was just finishing up a—"

"Get to work, or I'll fire you."

The girl shrugged. "First I have to put something away."

Ignoring Smythe's glare, she headed around the corner.

When Smythe saw me, his scowl deepened.

"Going to chase after that boy with glasses?" I asked conversationally.

He snorted. "The manager said to let him go. That's not how *I'd* deal with him."

"You'd set him on fire?"

I thought it was mildly amusing. But Smythe snapped, "The manager said you can go on the ride free. So go already."

"Wait," I said. "Tell me about the kid. Has her aunt reported her missing?"

Smythe widened his eyes. "Kid?"

Chapter Two

Smythe stomped back to the entrance. He started taking tickets again.

Kid? The guy was messing with me, like it was a joke. Meanwhile, some woman somewhere was out of her mind with worry about Blondie.

People shoved past. They were mad about the delay.

To let them by, I backed against the wall. I tossed my ball up and down. I thought of going back to the office, checking on Blondie. But if I did, I might miss out on the big drop. If I went up now, I could still make practice.

The manager would look after Blondie, I told myself. That was a manager's job. The kid would be okay.

I headed to the front of the line. Smythe nodded at me as I made my way inside.

"…the harder they fall!" the puppet jeered at me as I entered the passageway.

Around the first turn, a woman on a large screen welcomed us. She wore a floppy white hat, a white dress and a glittery silver necklace. The effect was blinding.

The woman said:

"I am Sherry Moore, Death Drop's designer and manager. I've always been fascinated by the myth of Persephone. The idea of someone falling into the underworld. All because she ate enchanted pomegranate seeds!"

Sherry paused for dramatic effect.

Two burly guys glanced at each other. "Ever eaten a pomegranate?" one asked.

The other replied, "Eaten one? I can't even *spell* it!"

They laughed loudly.

Sherry was saying, "Persephone's mother was Demeter, the goddess of agriculture. Demeter was heartbroken about losing Persephone for six months of the year. The goddess was so upset that she stopped things from growing.

"According to the ancient Greeks, that's why we have winter! All is cold, barren, lifeless while Demeter grieves for her stolen daughter."

The burly guys didn't think much of Sherry's spiel. "Bo-o-o-ring!" one of them complained.

"Yeah," agreed another. "We want some thrills. Some laughs. Not *this*."

They lumbered around the next curve.

"It's not boring at all," said a solemn voice.

I looked around. It was Dieter.

"Nothing about this place is boring," the Deet assured me. "Not the myth. Not her." He pointed to the screen.

"Oh yeah?" I tried not to sound overly interested. Once the Deet got started, it was hard to shut him up. That was another reason Coach yelled at Dieter to scram. The guy rattled off baseball stats nonstop. A regular walking Wikipedia.

Dieter explained, "Sherry has wealthy relatives in England. She talked them into lending her their painting of Persephone. It's brilliant, really. That painting is a rare early version of one of the most famous paintings in the world. Putting it in the center of this attraction means attracting educated art enthusiasts as well as thrill seekers. It's a bold move."

I whistled. "Not bad."

"One problem. Sherry isn't that great a businesswoman. In building Death Drop, she went way over budget. She owes a ton of money."

"How do you know all this stuff?" I demanded.

"I read about it in *Business Weekly*. I'm doing a report on Death Drop for camp."

"For *camp*? What happened to swimming and archery?"

The Deet adjusted his glasses. "This is Leaders of Tomorrow camp. My parents signed me up."

I had no words. I made a point of pulling out my cell phone to check the time.

"Ironic, isn't it?" Dieter commented.

I was already edging away.

"I mean, Persephone fell into the underworld," Dieter pointed out. "And Sherry fell into debt! Both of them ended up in a desperate situation."

"I know how they felt," I muttered—and walked quickly on.

"Hey, Zeke! Could you put in a word for me with Coach?" Dieter called after me.

I had other things to think about.

The floor beneath me was splitting in two. It pulled apart in jagged halves, with loud splintering sounds.

I jumped back just in time. The people ahead were trapped. Flames rushed up at them from the yawning chasm. Smoke billowed around them.

People screamed. One of the burly guys shrieked in terror.

But no one was falling. It was a glass floor. The flames, the chasm, were just images.

I sniffed. The smoke wasn't real. It came from one of those machines they use on movie sets. I glanced around. There it was, hanging from the ceiling.

The people ahead looked down. They saw their feet safely planted on the glass. They realized they weren't falling and relaxed.

The burly guy who'd shrieked now scowled. His buddy pointed at him. He yelped with laughter.

Like you weren't scared as well, I thought. I had to hand it to Death Drop's designer. Sherry had a wicked imagination. She could fool people.

I picked up my pace. I didn't want to be late for practice. I ran around the next turn—and into the red fake fruit of a large fake tree.

I got it. The hanging fruits were supposed to be pomegranates.

I pushed through them. Between two more fake trees, on a large screen, a video was playing. It showed a woman holding a pomegranate.

I didn't have to be brainy Deet to figure out who she was. It was Persephone.

With a knife, she sliced a wedge from the pomegranate, exposing the blood-red seeds. She pulled some seeds free and popped them into her mouth.

In a big puff of smoke, a black-cloaked man appeared. He had dark hair, deathly pale skin and pointed ears.

"I am Hades," he boomed. "You will become my wife. We will live forever in the underworld and never see sunlight again!"

"B-but I don't want to live in the underworld," Persephone objected.

Hades threw back his head. He laughed. His evil laughter rang on and on.

The screen turned dark. Someone in a demon outfit burst from behind a plastic tree. Waving his arms, he ran down the passage. "Bwa-ha-ha!"

His shouts were halfhearted. I didn't think he was really into it.

But a white-haired lady seemed to buy it. "This is too much!" she cried, clutching her chest. "I can't take the screams!"

"Bwa-ha-ha!" the guy in the demon outfit yelled again.

I wasn't sure *I* could take the bad acting.

The white-haired lady was still moaning. "I wasn't expecting this kind of shock…"

A sign outside the entrance warned anyone who had a weak heart not to ride Death Drop. I said, "Ma'am? Maybe you shouldn't continue up to the ride."

She managed a frail, sweet smile. "Not continue? And miss the painting? Oh no, dear."

Fanning herself with a Death Drop brochure, she trudged ahead.

A finger jabbed at my shoulder. It was Dieter.

He said, "The lady's right. You don't want to miss the portrait of Persephone. Especially since…"

He paused to straighten his glasses. "…*the portrait has a curse on it.*"

Chapter Three

Visitors crammed the next turn of the passage.

Dieter jumped up and down. "I can't see!"

I could. I'd always been the tallest kid in class. I gazed over people's heads to the portrait, in rich oil colors, of Persephone.

She was dressed in blue-gray silk. She had long, thick, dark hair.

She was holding a pomegranate with a slice taken out of it. Her blue eyes were sad, fearful—like she knew she'd made a big mistake.

Black curtains hung behind the portrait. A chain stretched in front to keep gawkers from getting too close. A security guard waved a hand to the right, up the passage. "Move along." He sounded bored.

A few people shifted away. The Deet still had to jump to see the portrait. It was like standing next to a grasshopper. Exasperated, I hoisted him up by the waist. "Here, Deet. Fill your eyes with Persephone and enjoy."

Dieter peered down at me solemnly. "To Dante Rossetti she wasn't Persephone. She was Proserpina, the ancient Roman version of Persephone. I hope you don't mind me correcting you, Zeke. These details are important."

All I knew about the ancient Romans was that they fed people to lions. Dieter and his details were starting to make me feel nostalgic for those days.

But I did let the Deet have a good long look before I set him down. "So tell me about the painting's curse."

Dieter beamed. Now he could get into full lecture mode.

"The artist who painted that portrait was Dante Gabriel Rossetti. Dante was in love with the woman who modeled for the painting. Like, he was *obsessed*. For years she was all Dante painted, portrait after portrait.

"But Dante's love for her was hopeless. She was married. Dante wasted away and died. His love was his curse."

With the edge of his T-shirt, Dieter cleaned his glasses. He blinked solemnly at me. "In the painting, you can see both sunlight and shadow. They say the sunlight represents Persephone's six months on earth when she's happy. The shadows stand for the half year she's stuck underground.

"The sunlight and shadow could also represent Dante's feelings for his model. He loved her, but he couldn't have her."

I tossed my ball up and down a few times. I thought about someone being that obsessed. I supposed I was obsessed too—about pitching.

At least my obsession got me out into the fresh air. "This Dan Rossetti guy spent too much time indoors," I said finally.

From the portrait, Persephone's sad blue eyes seemed to say:

Yeah? Imagine being stuck underground for six months!

Trailing blood-red juice, a pomegranate rolled through the air at me. Other holograms spun by, fast as bowling balls. Drumrolls completed the effect.

A neon sign on the wall welcomed us to the next part of the tower: *EVER THOUGHT ABOUT BEING BURIED ALIVE?*

With a thunderous grinding noise, the ceiling descended toward us.

Some people ran out of the ever-narrowing space. Others ducked or sat. They gazed up, hypnotized, as the ceiling closed in on us.

I crouched. The Deet and I looked at each other. We laughed, partly out of nervousness. We knew this ceiling wasn't the real one. It was a special effect. We weren't actually going to be crushed.

It was one powerful illusion.

A little too powerful, as it turned out, for the white-haired lady.

She fainted.

The ceiling stopped. A demon's face flashed across it. His yellow eyes glittered down at us. He burst into chilling laughter.

The ceiling receded. It hadn't even lowered to Dieter's height.

The old lady was too far gone to realize that. I knelt beside her. She was moaning.

I started to help her up.

Smythe struggled through the crowd. He elbowed me aside. "I'll handle this," he snapped. "I'm trained in first aid."

Smythe helped the woman up— exactly like I'd been doing.

I glanced around for security cameras. I didn't see any. How had he known about the woman? And got here so fast?

Funeral-type organ music blasted from all sides. The dim light turned red. Round red glitter poured from the ceiling, a storm of pomegranate seeds.

"We have to get this lady out of here," I told Smythe.

Through the glitter he frowned at me. His message was clear—*Butt out.* The woman sagged against him, more rag doll than human. She might faint again. She'd need two of us to support her.

Smythe punched a number into his cell phone. "Guard! Area-four emergency!"

"I think I'm going to be sick," the woman said between moans. She pulled a large handkerchief from her purse and pressed it over her mouth.

I said, "Don't worry, ma'am."

The security guard muscled through. He put his arm around the woman. Smythe stepped aside.

The woman noticed everyone staring at her. She started mumbling. It was hard to hear through that big hankie. I bent close.

She mumbled, "Need my doctor…"

Smythe said, "I'll go hail a cab. The guard will help you out."

He pushed quickly through the crowd.

The woman was coughing into her handkerchief. The guard began guiding her away. She stumbled, cried out.

"It's okay," the guard told her. "We'll take it nice and slow."

Everyone was silent, watching. Smythe paused. He glanced back at the woman. He ran his tongue over his teeth.

I didn't blame him for being worried. But his plan sucked. He should have called medics and a stretcher to come up here. Not forced the old lady to walk all the way down.

There was something weird about Smythe. Something...*desperate*.

What was with him? If you operated an amusement ride, you should be— well, amused. Having a good time.

Smythe wasn't even pretending to have fun.

And where was the manager? Sitting with her feet up on her desk in the office?

The office. I backtracked my thoughts. Blondie.

I thought Blondie's aunt must have shown up by now. The kid would be away from here, safe with her family.

Wouldn't she?

Dieter and I rounded the last curve. We reached the lineup for the elevator. For the big drop.

The elevator's black doors stood open. An attendant wearing a red hood with horned ears ushered people in. It was the same dude who had run through the passageway with the unconvincing evil laugh.

He was warning each person, "Death Drop falls at forty miles an hour. It's quite a shock. Are you ready for that?"

It must have been some safety thing—that he had to make sure each passenger knew what they were getting into. The delay gave the rest of us time to look around the tower's top floor.

It was a forest scene. A winding path led up to a cliff, which curved out over an abyss. A Persephone mannequin stood at the edge of the cliff. She had thick dark hair and wore blue-gray silk, like in the painting.

She also held—surprise, surprise—a pomegranate. An eerie red light shone out of it.

"The moral?" joked Dieter. "Always buy organic."

His voice was a bit shaky though. The scene was getting to him.

Wind blew through Persephone's hair and rustled the leaves of the fake trees. I squinted into the darkness behind her. I made out some boulders spaced a few feet apart. I figured a wind machine was hidden behind them.

In the gray-painted sky, lightning flared and thunder cracked.

From the abyss, flames surged up. They turned into clawlike fingers that reached for Persephone.

A scream rang out.

"Help! I'm trapped! I'm going to burn up!"

Dieter and I looked at each other. The scream must be another special effect. Persephone, shrieking for rescue.

It didn't make sense though. In the myth, Hades didn't want to deep-fry Persephone. He wanted her alive and well, to be his wife.

Another scream followed, louder and more desperate.

"You idiots! Listen to me—*this is not part of the show!*"

Chapter Four

I'd know that whiny voice anywhere. It was Smythe's. He was in trouble.

A chain strung between several metal posts separated the lineup from the forest. I jumped over the chain. I ran to the top of the cliff.

The whole structure was lightweight. It shook but didn't break.

"You can't go there!" shouted the attendant.

I ignored him. I was busy dodging fake trees. As the structure quaked, they were falling over.

Persephone was wobbling too. I caught the mannequin before it fell. I straightened it up.

I looked over the cliff. It was about fifteen feet down. The flames had sunk back into their circle of jets. They must be on a timer. At some point soon, they'd surge up again.

From straight below I heard a loud creak—then a thud.

"Smythe?" I called.

It was dark down there. But I could see well enough to know nobody was there. Nobody alive—and nobody burned to a crisp either.

There was just the circle of jets. Also, stacked against the far wall, some spare fake boulders.

Red Cape charged up behind me. "You trying to get me in trouble? I'm supposed to keep order around here."

Through the hood's slits, his eyes gazed at me unhappily. I felt bad for him.

On the other hand, it was hard to take someone with red, horned ears too seriously.

I pointed out, "I heard Smythe scream for help. Don't pretend you didn't."

Red Cape sighed. "Yeah, I heard. It's just another special effect. Sherry keeps dreaming up new ones. She loves this smoke-and-mirrors stuff."

"You should tell Sherry to ditch this effect," I advised. "It's not getting barbecued that Persephone is worried about. It's missing out on sunlight for six months."

The attendant's shoulders slumped. "I know how Persephone feels. I hate this job. It's so dark in here. So depressing. Next summer, I'm applying for something outdoors."

With a heavy sigh, he started straightening up the fallen trees. I helped him.

We trudged down the cliff. People in the lineup glared at us. Now that they knew everything was okay, they wanted to go on the ride. They wanted to experience Death Drop.

The Deet and I reached the elevator. The attendant stared at Dieter. "No way y*ou're* going on the ride."

"He's doing this for homework," I said. "Business camp." I pushed Dieter inside, right to the back.

The attendant gave one of his heavy sighs. I could guess his thoughts. He should do his job. He should wade in and bodily remove the Deet.

But the next people were eager to get on. The attendant left us alone.

He checked that everyone was sitting and safety-belted. Then he bellowed, "And now—to your doom!"

He crashed the red-splattered doors shut.

The elevator dropped sharply—then jolted to a halt. Dieter clutched his stomach. Girls screamed.

Slowly everyone relaxed. That first drop had been a joke. A false alarm.

The elevator darkened. On each wall, the portrait of Persephone appeared.

Even in the dim light you could see how beautiful she was. But the sadness in her eyes was missing. They were just beautiful blue eyes with no expression.

It was a copy of the portrait.

It blurred, turned into a cartoon. Persephone's lips moved. Her eyes blazed.

"Don't make the mistake I did," she warned. "Don't take a bite of the pomegranate. Or else…"

She leaned forward. "*Or else you will take the Death Drop.* The one-way trip to the underworld!"

The elevator gave a violent lurch. People swayed. It was like being sloshed around in a giant teacup.

Persephone's mouth opened wide. She let out a blood-curdling scream.

The elevator plunged.

Persephone disappeared. The top half of the elevator slid back. We were hurtling down, down into gigantic flames.

Beyond the flames, in a sickly orange blur, we saw skyscrapers, Burrard Inlet, the mountains beyond. The deeper we fell, the more the landscape seemed to melt into the fire.

Most of the passengers were yelling in terror. Everyone's hair flew up.

I pressed my back against the seat. With the force of the drop, my skin was pulling away from my bones. My face felt like it was about to peel off.

I gritted my teeth. I forced myself to stay calm. The drop was just one more of Sherry's illusions. Making you think something was happening that wasn't.

Even belted in, Dieter was sliding up in his seat. The guy was too light for the ride.

"Help! Help!" he yelled.

I had to laugh. "You should have paid attention to—"

The cardboard demon, I meant to say. But then Death Drop slowed. It coasted gently to the ground.

Around us, the flames vanished. Sunshine and blue sky surrounded us.

Everyone staggered out. Some were laughing. Some looked ill. One of the burly guys made a dash for the men's room.

I glanced around for Dieter. He was still in his seat. He was pale but determined. He said hoarsely, "I'm staying on.

I'm going back up. I want another look at the portrait."

The elevator soared to the top of the tower.

People were filing into the Death Drop souvenir shop. Persephone dolls smiled out of display cases. Also for sale were demon-face key chains and flame-shaped chocolates.

A Death Drop poster was tacked up on the wall. It showed an elevator-load of screaming people plunging into a fiery pit.

A girl with dark-red hair was twirling a long metal tube like a baton. She was the girl I'd seen earlier. Smythe had snapped at her to get to work.

The girl called out, "Share the fun! With our special mailing tubes, you can send the Death Drop poster to a friend!"

She saw my expression and grinned. She must have guessed my thoughts— what a lame gift those posters would be.

I liked how her bright green eyes had laughter in them. "Still taking notes?" I asked.

"I wasn't taking notes, pitcher boy."

"Oh yeah? Then what—?"

But a customer asked to see a Persephone doll, and she had to help. I walked out of the shop, into the sun.

The sidewalk was crammed with vendor stalls. Hot dogs, ice cream, balloons, candy floss. Even sketches, spread out on the sidewalk.

Across the road, my teammates were gathering on the baseball diamond.

Practice was about to start.

But first I had to check on Blondie. I needed to know that she'd found her aunt. That she wasn't sitting scared and alone in the office.

Coach came out of the park club-house. He spotted me. That was the problem with being tall. It was hard to hide.

He waved, beckoned me over.

I was an ace pitcher. A "stellar" one, to use Coach's term.

Coach thought highly of me. Like I said, he was probably going to recommend me for a university scholarship.

If I didn't get on his bad side. If I didn't show up late for a practice. Lateness was not stellar, he often reminded us.

I glanced at the entrance to Death Drop. At Smythe, taking people's tickets.

Just past him, inside, was the office.

Blondie's accusing little face floated into my mind. And her stubby finger, pointing at my baseball shirt. *Angels help people.*

I slammed my baseball into my palm a few times. "I'm not that type of angel," I muttered.

I'd said that to Blondie. It hadn't made any difference to her. Now it wasn't making any difference to me either.

Coach or no Coach, I had to see if she'd found her aunt.

Chapter Five

It would take me five minutes, tops, to check. Coach wouldn't refuse me a college recommendation for five minutes.

I jogged over to Smythe.

"I want to check on Blond—uh, that kid who lost her aunt."

He scowled. "You just want to get in for a second free ride. You'll have to buy a ticket and stand in line. Like everyone else."

Behind Smythe was a second cardboard demon. This one was missing its face. People could put their own face in the hole and get their photo snapped.

I raised my arm and aimed. I lobbed my baseball over Smythe's shoulder and through the cutout's hole.

"Oops, lost my ball," I said. I ducked under the rope and ran in. I ignored Smythe's protests.

Grabbing the ball, I marched to the office door.

The elevator attendant sprawled in the chair I'd left Blondie sitting in. He was swigging a Coke, his red cape and hood in his lap. He was on break.

He belched, then sighed. "You again. I hope you're not going to start knocking chairs over or something."

I looked around the office. He was alone. "I wanted to make sure the blond kid found her aunt."

"What blond kid?"

Smythe's voice echoed in my brain. *Kid?*

Bad jokes shouldn't be told once, let alone repeated.

I stared hard at the attendant. He was puzzled. He really didn't know what I was talking about.

He said, "You better get out before Smythe calls the police."

I leaned on the counter. "Let's do that. Let's call 9-1-1," I invited. "It's time the cops got here."

The attendant heaved another sigh. "All I wanted was a few minutes' quiet. A few minutes free of screamers, flames and darkness. Why can't you leave me alone? What have I ever done to you?"

He punched in more than three numbers. He wasn't calling the police.

"Ms. Moore? I'm in the office. There's somebody here you need to deal with. The guy who tried to wreck the display."

He listened for a moment. His face grew unhappier. He replaced the phone. "I'm to keep you here till the guard arrives," he announced glumly.

I spotted a door at the end of the wall. I walked over to it.

"Hey! You can't go in there! You're supposed to wait."

I opened the door. It led into the souvenir shop. The sales clerk was twirling her baton. "With our metal mailing tubes, you can send posters to—"

She stopped when she saw me. She laughed. She remembered what I'd thought about the posters.

I grinned back. She was a refreshing change. Unlike the other Death Drop staff, she was cheerful.

Plus she had those green eyes.

I asked, "You didn't see a lost blond kid wander through, did you?"

The clerk shook her head. "The only thing out of the usual was a frail old lady. She looked sick. She had a handkerchief pressed to her mouth. She staggered out to a taxi. I wanted to help her, but she waved me off."

I couldn't believe it. "The old lady was on her own? Smythe wasn't with her? Somebody should send Smythe on the big drop—without the elevator."

The clerk didn't look too upset at the idea. Then she frowned, as if remembering something. She started to speak.

Somebody tapped me on the shoulder. The Deet. He babbled, "So guess what. I went back to the portrait. Got a second look. And this time? It was a letdown!"

I didn't get the chance to ask why. The security guard lumbered over. I shrugged apologetically at the clerk. Whatever she'd been about to say would have to wait. The gift shop was turning into my own personal Grand Central Station.

The guard shoved his face up to mine. "Edwin tells me we need to have a talk."

Edwin. That would be the hooded attendant.

"It's about time someone listened to me," I told the guard. "I've been trying to find out about—"

"I don't think you get my meaning, wise guy. *I'm* going to talk to *you*."

The security guard peeled off his *Death Drop Security* jacket. He rolled it up and stuffed it under his arm like it was a sleeping bag. "Hot day," he explained.

He stomped outside to a bench. I followed. Not that the guy was my idea of a great companion. I thought maybe I could get through to him.

Across the street, Coach gave a massive, sarcastic shrug. I could guess his thoughts. The team was starting practice, and I was busy chatting. Not stellar.

The guard noticed Coach's shrug. It would be hard not to. Coach was a big guy. The shrug had been like the shifting of a tectonic plate.

The guard sat back. He laced his fingers behind his head. "I used to play baseball," he said conversationally.

"That's great," I replied. "But what about—"

"I was an outfielder," the guard said. "Loved the game. Never missed a practice."

I wasn't interested in hearing his baseball memoirs. I tossed my ball up and down. I forced my voice to stay even.

"Sir, I'm really worried about this blond kid. She told me her aunt was missing. She—"

Smiling, the guard shook his head at me. "We have no missing-child report. No hysterical aunt on the phone."

He leaned forward. "Smythe never saw any blond kid. He says you and a smart aleck with glasses jumped the line. He says you made up this lost-kid story to embarrass them, in case…"

His eyes bored into mine. "…in case the Death Drop manager files a police complaint about the two of you."

"That's crazy! Smythe's lying! He—"

"Now, now. No need to shout."

I spotted Dieter. He was holding a huge candy-floss cone. He was peeking from behind it to watch us. He was playing spy.

I shut my eyes for a moment to keep them from rolling.

The guard was back to his memoirs. "Like I said, when I was your age, I was an outfielder. And I *never missed a practice.*"

I clenched my baseball. What did the guy want, a medal?

He lowered his voice. Now we were buddies, sharing a secret. "I see what happened. That's your team over there. It's a practice day. But the field is right across from Death Drop. The thrill ride everyone's talking about.

"You can't resist. You just have to go on Death Drop. But it means you're going to be late. You're going to be in trouble with your coach."

The guard winked. "So…you make up a story about a lost kid."

"I didn't make her up."

The guard frowned. He whipped out his security-guard badge. "Don't mess with me. I may not be a cop, but I have the right to detain you. If the manager would let me, I'd phone the cops."

I didn't know about this detain stuff. But I did know that the badge, seen from across the street, could just as well be a police one. In his jeans and T, the guard could be an undercover cop.

Sure enough, Coach and my teammates were staring at us. My teammates' mouths hung open.

It must have been a sight to see their pitcher being questioned, possibly arrested.

Coach looked surprised and angry.

No, *angry* didn't quite capture it. Thunderous. That was it.

And I saw my scholarship prospects fluttering away in pieces, like the pomegranate-shaped glitter.

Chapter Six

When the guard went back inside, Dieter hurried up to me.

"Don't you have a home?" I asked irritably.

My mood had, if it was even possible, gotten worse. I'd received a text from Coach that said, **Forget coming 2 practice. Meet me @ the park @ 6. Ur explanation better be STELLAR.**

I glanced across the street. Coach was in a huddle with my teammates.

I wondered if my ears should be burning.

The Deet peered solemnly up at me. "I waited around to see if I could help."

I stared at Dieter. "Hey, *you* didn't see Blondie, did you? I took her to the manager's office when you were barging into Death Drop."

Dieter shook his head. "I was in a hurry. I wanted to see the painting of Persephone. I'll never forget that first view I had of it! Wow."

He brightened. "I could *say* I saw the kid."

"No. We have enough liars. We need to find someone who will tell the truth."

Dieter phoned his mom to say he'd be home a bit late. "I'm hanging out with a baseball pitcher."

I heard a delighted gasp. Then his mom gushed, "Oh, honey, you've made a *friend*? I'm so happy! I just knew one day those baseball boys would realize how special you are."

Dieter flushed. I gazed ahead, pretending I couldn't hear.

His mom said warmly, "You be home when you can, Dieter. Not too late, mind." A happy laugh tinkled out of the phone. "It's just so sweet that they're paying attention to you!"

She rang off. I noticed the Deet's dejected face. I thought of him showing up at practices. Begging Coach to let him play. Rattling off baseball stats to prove he knew the game.

Dieter's mom meant well. But it wasn't sweetness Dieter wanted. It wasn't people thinking he was special.

He wanted to play baseball.

I gave Dieter a friendly arm punch, then surveyed the Death Drop line.

All I needed was one honest person. Hadn't some philosopher said that, way back? In my case, one honest person who had seen Blondie. Who would say I wasn't lying.

Lots of people had been around when Blondie walked up to me. It would have been hard not to hear her crying and complaining. But those people were long gone. The ones in the lineup were all new arrivals.

Or maybe not. There might be some repeat riders.

I looked at the Deet. "How about if you go up and down the line, asking people if they were here earlier this afternoon. If they remember a little girl with blond, sausage-shaped curls."

It was a rotten favor to ask the Deet. People in line on a hot day were cranky. He'd get some rude responses. Some flipped fingers.

But he nodded, his glasses bobbing on his nose.

"I'll pay you back," I promised. "I'm going to teach you how to throw."

Dieter's jaw dropped. It hung there as he tried to process what I'd said. Finally he spluttered, "Me—*throw?* Wow!"

"Sure," I said. "It's not like you can't be scholarly *and* athletic. Not if someone practices with you."

I headed for the vendor at the far end, whose sign promised *DEVILISHLY GOOD CANDY FLOSS!* The stall was topped by a picture of a demon gobbling a pink swirl of floss.

A mom and two kids stood grinning in front of the stall. The dad was filming them.

Behind me, footsteps pounded the sidewalk.

It was Smythe. He was waving his arms and shouting.

"Get out! You have no right to be here!"

This was a public sidewalk. Nobody had the right to keep me off it. Especially not a liar-liar-pants-on-fire.

I stepped forward to say that to Smythe.

But he ran by. He hadn't even seen me. It was the dad with the videocam Smythe was yelling at.

Past the candy-floss stall, a limo had just pulled up to the curb. Smythe didn't want the dad filming the limo.

Looking offended, the family retreated. When they were a safe distance away, one of the kids shouted that Smythe was a moron.

Well, yeah.

Meanwhile, a chauffeur opened one of the passenger doors. A woman in a white dress, floppy hat and flashy diamond jewelry got out.

I held my hand over my eyes. I'd had this blinding experience before. It was the woman from the video. Sherry Moore, manager and designer of Death Drop.

She was finally showing up for the day.

Smythe rushed over to Sherry. His pinched face took on a sucky, adoring look. He told her everything was fine.

Sherry nodded impatiently. She walked toward Death Drop, her high heels making loud *clip-clop*s on the pavement. Smythe had to scurry to keep up.

It hit me. Sherry didn't like Smythe. I bet the manager saw right through him. Right into his inner weasel.

That gave me hope. Sherry might listen to me. After all, as manager she was responsible for what happened at Death Drop.

I ran up to her. "Hey, ma'am, I need to talk to you. It's about the blond kid who lost her aunt. Smythe phoned you about her. But now he says the kid never existed."

Even with all that sun-flashing jewelry in the way, I could see the manager was startled. She shot a look at Smythe. "What's all this about?"

Smythe whispered in her ear. Sherry shot me a distrustful glance. She let Smythe bustle her into Death Drop.

That decided it for me. Somehow I had to talk to Sherry Moore—on my own and Smythe-less.

you have this kind of experi-
?"

experience?"

g people nobody else does."

look I gave him, Dieter
several steps. "I'm not saying
ieve you. Honest, I—*oof!*"
acked into the cushion stall.
ushion lady chirped, "My
dys imagined people. Always
visible friends, she was!"

't imagine things," I muttered.
id I? A doubt floated in my
aybe everybody was right.
ad imagined Blondie.

to push the idea away by
more sketches. Here was a
spinning as he directed traffic.
a wide-eyed baby watching a
And here…

ubt in my mind dissolved. I
a wide grin.

Chapter Seven

I had no chance of seeing the manager now. If I tried barging into Death Drop, Smythe would call the security guard.

Dieter was questioning the people in line. The day was getting hotter. His glasses kept sliding down his nose, and he kept pushing them back up.

I figured I might as well do my bit. I headed back to the candy-floss stall.

The vendor was a woman with fluffy platinum hair. She twinkled at me. "Lemon? Raspberry? Grape? Bubblegum? Apple cinn—"

"No, thanks," I said before she could rhyme off any more flossy flavors. I described Blondie. I asked if the vendor had seen her.

"A kid with sausage curls? Not that I noticed." She patted her own fluffy 'do, possibly to check that it hadn't fallen off.

I went to the next vendor, and the next, right to the end. Nobody had noticed Blondie. The popcorn vendor was snarky about it. He pointed out that there were billions of blond kids on Earth.

The hot-dog guy overheard and felt sorry for me. He gave me a container of free fries. But no, he hadn't seen Blondie.

"Me neither, hon," said the next vendor. Her stall had red-velvet cushions

embroidere
face.

Beside th
thick, cream
the sidewalk
pink piggy
please pay by
a donation, j

I notice
were. How
cherry bloss
face and wa
seagull stan
one leg.

I check
corner of t
artist's nan
drawing of
My pho
Coach. **The**
explanation

Dieter r
Blondie." H

at me. "L
ence ofte
"Wha
"Seei
At th
retreated
I don't be
He'd
The
auntie Gl
one for ir
"I don
Or…
mind. M
Maybe I
I trie
looking
cop, arms
And here
butterfly.
I stare
The d
broke int

The cushion lady was in full memory mode. "They ended up putting Auntie Gladys away. That's what happens when you can't tell what's real and what isn't!"

"I wouldn't know, ma'am," I replied.

I felt in my back pocket for my wallet. I stuffed a ten into the piggy bank. I picked up the sketch.

Which showed Blondie yelling, a stubby finger pointing—at me.

Dieter ogled the sketch. "Whoa," he breathed. "Sorry about the imaginary-people remark."

With my cell phone, I snapped a photo of the sketch. I wasn't taking any chances. I wanted a backup copy.

I rolled up the sketch and put it in my backpack. I checked the time on my phone. Almost five. I needed to talk to the artist. He or she would be back to collect the money and unsold sketches. Sometime.

I couldn't wait. I had proof that Blondie existed. I had to show it to Sherry Moore.

The all-too-familiar problem leered at me like the demon puppet. *How to get inside?* Smythe wouldn't fall for my lost-ball routine a second time. He'd yell the house down.

I could go through the souvenir shop. I didn't think the green-eyed sales clerk would start screaming. If anything, she'd laugh.

However, to get in through the shop, I'd have to jump over the exit turnstile. That would attract a whole lot of attention. The guard would be on me before I got a chance to talk to Sherry.

I needed to get in without anyone seeing.

Dieter was studying the cushions. He traced the rhinestones sewn around Persephone's neck. "The Rossetti painting doesn't show Persephone with a neck-lace," he told the cushion lady.

The vendor grabbed the cushion from him crossly. She set it in its place again.

Something gleamed on the side of the cushion. A zipper.

The red velvet was just a cover. Removable.

"I take great pride in my cushions," the vendor was saying in an injured tone. "I lovingly hand-sew each one…"

She kept yakking, but I didn't hear. I was picturing the cushion cover—removed. Turned inside out so Persephone wasn't showing.

I bought one of the cushions. I unzipped the cover and took it off. I handed the cushion back to the aston-ished vendor. "Thanks. I won't be needing this."

With my penknife, I scored two slits in the cover to see through.

The vendor wailed, "What are you doing? My beautiful creation!"

I walked around behind the stall. I pulled the cushion cover over my head. Hooded, I'd fit right in at Death Drop.

Because I'd got it wrong just now. I didn't have to get in without anyone seeing.

I had to get in without anyone seeing *me*.

Chapter Eight

Dieter peered owlishly up at me. "I'm to be your decoy."

"Yeah. If you run in, they won't notice me."

"But I—"

"You'll get to see the Persephone portrait again."

"Two times was enough. The thrill wore off."

"Dude. Smythe is lying about Blondie. I have to tell the manager."

Dieter sighed. "Oh, all *right*."

He ran to Death Drop's entrance. He ducked under the rope, right in front of Smythe.

Smythe lunged.

But Dieter was too fast. The guy was like quicksilver. He vanished up the passageway.

Smythe punched numbers on a cell phone. Busy whining into it, he didn't notice me slip under the rope.

I pulled my new hood over my face. I ran after the Deet.

Dieter and I met up by Sherry Moore's video. We and several other people held up our hands to ward off the glare from her jewelry.

Then—

The real Sherry burst around the corner.

I waved at her. This was my chance. I'd tell her about Blondie.

Sherry saw me. Her flashy-ringed hands pushed people aside. She waded through. She was smiling. Things were going to go well.

Okay, so there was a speck-sized chance they wouldn't. Just in case, I gave my phone to Dieter. "If Sherry doesn't believe me, get out of here. My coach will be in the park across the street at six. My password is *strikeout*. Show the sketch to him. Explain what's happened."

Sherry reached us. She winked at me. I felt a rush of relief. I'd been right about the manager. She was okay.

Before I could speak, Sherry turned to Dieter. The smile disappeared. She clamped her jeweled fingers on Dieter's shoulders.

She snarled, "You have trespassed once too often."

Not a good start. But once I explained—

"We're looking for a sausage," Dieter blurted. "I mean, a blond sausage. A missing one. I mean…"

He was babbling. He was terrified, in shock.

Through her thick red lipstick, Sherry hissed, "There is no missing child. There never was."

I gave Dieter's ear a sharp twist.

"Yeowch!" He twisted out of Sherry's grip to glare at me. He wasn't in shock now. He was mad.

I gave him a shove. As in, *This is your chance. Go*.

His eyes widened. He got it. Sherry was reaching for him again. But, bending low, he burrowed through the crowd.

Seconds—and a few startled screams—later, the Deet emerged at the edge of the crowd. He dashed down the passage, toward the entrance, a natural escape artist. Persephone could have used his skills.

Under her heavy face powder, Sherry was red with fury. She whipped around to me.

No way I could slip away like Dieter. I was too tall.

There was one thing I could do anyway.

"Ma'am, this is my fault, not that boy's," I said.

Sherry said tersely, "Don't blame yourself, Edwin. You tried to stop him. You did your best."

The hood—I'd forgotten I was wearing it!

My idea had worked. Sherry thought I was the elevator guy.

Sherry snapped, "Well, don't just stand there. Get back to your post!"

I didn't need convincing. I shoved through the crowd and up the passage.

As I recalled, the real Edwin wasn't as tall as I was. I didn't want to give Sherry a chance to notice that.

Around the next curve, I ran into the fake pomegranates. In the video playing on the wall, Persephone was sobbing her heart out.

People were glancing at me. It was the hood. They were expecting theatrics. An evil laugh or something.

I pulled the hood off. I wanted to blend in.

In the video, a demonic figure loomed over Persephone.

I'd seen it, heard it all before.

But *had* I?

Last time I was here, Edwin had run down the passage with his hokey evil laugh. It looked like he'd come from around the next turn.

But the Persephone portrait was around the next turn. Gawkers crammed that part of the passage. There was no way Edwin could have run through such a tightly packed crowd.

He must have come from some-where else. Somewhere with the space to work up a good sprint.

I looked around. And got another face full of fake pomegranates.

Last time, I'd passed the pomegran-ates. The video was the attraction. The video got people's attention.

Now, I waded right into the pomegranates.

So *many* pomegranates.

Such great camouflage.

I stuck my hands out in front of me. Blinded by the masses of plastic fruit, I didn't want to smash into a wall.

The pomegranates ended. Now I was on a slim stretch of floor behind them. This was where Edwin had got his running start.

I started walking. I came to black curtains. On the other side hung Rossetti's portrait.

I heard people's whispers. "Wow… So beautiful…So sad…"

"Move along," called the security guard, in the same bored voice.

For me, there wasn't room to move. I'd come to a wall. A dark dead end.

Wait. It wasn't totally dark. A thread of light ran along the base of the wall.

It was a door!

I felt for a handle. Found it. Turned it.

I saw a small round room.

Under a lamp, in a big stuffed chair, sat Blondie.

She frowned at me over the book of fairy tales she was reading. "Where have you *been?*"

Chapter Nine

"Where have *I* been? You're the one who vanished!"

Blondie shrugged. The sausage curls bounced. "Smythe brought me here. Aunt Sherry's orders."

My overworked brain struggled with this. Sherry Moore, manager of Death Drop. The kid's aunt.

Sherry had wealthy relatives in England. Blondie must be from that branch of the family.

I also remembered, in the office, Smythe swooping down on Blondie. *He'd known who she was.*

I shook my head at Blondie. Amazing how a kid could be so cute and so exasperating. "You didn't tell me your aunt was the manager."

She pushed out her lower lip. "You didn't ask me."

I looked around. There was a small refrigerator, and a coffeemaker with a box of cookies on top. Beside a narrow cupboard door, rolled-up posters and plastic bags of metal mailing tubes were piled up. There was also a box labeled *Persephone dolls*.

Blondie said, "It was all Aunt Sherry's fault. She left me to play in here. I got bored, Angel! I searched for her. I went outside. But she was gone."

Blondie frowned. "When Aunt Sherry invited me from London for a visit, she told my parents there was a lot to see in Vancouver. It would be good for me, she said. But I haven't seen *anything*."

Her mouth was trembling. I felt bad for her. I said, "Maybe some day you'll come back with someone who…"

Who actually notices you, I was about to say. I changed it to "Who has time to see the sights with you."

The kid pointed at a large brass trunk by the wall. "Aunt Sherry packed my things. She's taking me home to England. We leave soon."

A metal mailing tube lay on top of the trunk. Lifting it, I sank down on the trunk. I thought of the trouble Blondie had caused me. The hefty chance I'd be tossed off the team.

Not that it was Blondie's fault. It was Sherry's, for neglecting the kid. And Smythe's fault, too, for pretending

Blondie didn't exist. What was *that* about?

Why bother bringing the kid to Vancouver in the first place?

I wished I had my baseball to toss up and down. But the ball was in my backpack. So instead I balanced one end of the tube on my palm. It's always good to develop new skills.

"What's your name?" I asked.

"Gracie Moore." She brightened. "And you are my angel."

I remembered Coach's text, demanding that I meet him at six. With an explanation that *better be STELLAR.*

"Not an angel to everyone," I said. I'd been holding the mailing tube in my right hand. I shifted the tube to my left hand and held out my right. "Zeke Sheldon."

She shook my hand solemnly. "Zeke? I'm hungry."

I felt in a side pocket. I had a crushed, half-eaten chocolate bar. I handed it to her. She crammed it into her mouth. I got a chocolaty-toothed smile.

I stood up. She was okay. I should go. I needed to find Coach. Make a groveling apology. Offer to wash his suv for the next ten years.

But Sherry and Smythe were stuck in my mind like a mental chicken bone.

Why had they pretended Gracie didn't exist?

I was still holding the tube. Gracie pointed to it. "There's a Death Drop poster inside that," she said, mouth full of chocolate. "It's a souvenir for me. From Aunt Sherry."

I recalled the poster on display in the shop. The people on the elevator, screaming as they plunged into flames.

Bizarre gift for a little girl.

Then, on the other side of the door, we heard voices.

Gracie gaped at me in blue-eyed dismay. "It's Aunt Sherry and Smythe!"

I'd sneaked back in to find the manager. To show her the sketch of Gracie and me.

But that was before I knew what had happened to Gracie. Now I knew she was fine. I had no excuse for trespassing.

Sherry would be on the phone to the police faster than you could say *reform school*.

The door handle was turning. I had to hide. Where? I did a rapid three-sixty. Brassbound trunk. Piled-up tubes, posters, dolls.

Cupboard door.

I wrenched the handle, pulled the door open, jumped into—

Not a cupboard. A narrow spiral staircase.

Missing the first steps, my feet met air. I crashed onto my side. I slid down the endless stairs.

Chapter Ten

As I slid, the step edges crunched into my ribs. It was like having my rib cage played by a harpist. One with killer fingernails.

I jammed the soles of my runners against the wall. I stopped my fall.

I sat up, stretched out my legs. I breathed in deeply. I felt a jabbing pain in my ribs on the side I'd fallen on.

I wondered if I'd broken those ribs. I didn't think so. I'd broken my ribs a couple of years before. I'd been diving for third base in a steal.

This was painful, but not as bad as I remembered from that time.

I stood. These must be the employee stairs, with exits on each level.

I started down them.

Then—

Light poured through the winding shaft. Sherry called sharply, "Who's there?"

Sherry had heard me falling.

I stayed still. A few steps up, the light gleamed on something silver.

The metal mailing tube! I'd dropped it in my ungraceful downward skid.

If Sherry stepped into the stairwell and saw the tube, she might come to get it. I'd have to run. The way my ribs ached, I didn't feel like a sprint right now.

I caught her words—"Thought I heard something."

I heard the door shut.

I couldn't leave the tube there. Someone might trip over it. I climbed back up, grabbed it.

Sherry had left the tube on top of the trunk. All ready for when they left to catch their plane.

Except that I'd taken it.

Would Sherry notice it was missing?

No. A cheapo gift like that?

She might not notice.

But if she *did* notice…

If she was the eagle-eyed type…

I punched the end of the tube into my palm. I heard the poster *thunk* inside. I didn't like what I was thinking. Sherry might grill Gracie about the missing tube. Force her to admit someone had been up there.

Me.

Poor kid. I didn't want to get her in trouble.

I had to get the tube back on top of the trunk.

As I climbed back up the stairs, I heard Sherry's calm, voice through the door.

"I don't know why you're panicking, Smythe. So a couple of boys sneaked into Death Drop. One of them saw Gracie. The guard handled it."

I was by the door now. Smythe's whiny tones floated through. "The kid with glasses got away."

Dieter had escaped! *Yes!* I gave an air punch.

Sherry said, "Forget it, Smythe. We're almost done. So stop worrying and admire the view!"

Slowly, cautiously, I opened the door a crack and peeked through.

Sherry was looking out toward Lions Gate Bridge. "I'll miss Vancouver.

So lovely. So profitable!" Her rather shrill laugh rang out.

Smythe ran his tongue over his teeth. "You won't forget me, Sherry? I mean, I was the one who—"

"Smythe!" Sherry said sharply. Whatever he'd been about to say, Sherry did not want the kid to hear it.

Sherry glanced at her niece. But Gracie was deep into her book.

What *had* Smythe been going to say? He was the one who…what?

Sherry spoke again. "Of course I won't forget you, Smythe. You will be well taken care of."

Smythe nodded. He relaxed. He looked out the window.

And for that instant, Sherry allowed herself a smile. Not a friendly one. A mean *gotcha!* one. Cold enough to chip ice from.

Gracie glanced up from her book. She saw me. Her mouth made an O.

I winked at her. I lifted the metal mailing tube.

The kid glanced at the brassbound trunk. She saw the tube was missing.

I raised the tube like a spear. I could throw it to Gracie.

No! she mouthed. She pointed at the tube.

I looked at the tube in proper light for the first time since I—and it—had taken our little tumble down the stairs.

One end was dented.

Sherry would want to know why. I couldn't risk that. Somehow I had to get another mailing tube on top of that trunk.

"Think of all the things you will be able to buy," Sherry was telling Smythe. She studied his pale complexion. "You could go to a tanning salon."

Smythe winced. I almost felt sorry for him. It wasn't like he could help being pale.

My gaze fell on the tubes stacked against the wall. I reached out, picked one up. That was easy enough.

It felt lighter than the one I'd dropped. It must not have a poster inside. I wondered if Sherry would notice when she picked it up.

And suppose she opened it? She might want to make sure it was the right tube. One with a poster inside, not an empty tube.

I had to put one of those posters in the tube.

But I had a problem. The posters were bundled in bags of plastic. If I tried to pull one out, the plastic would make noise.

Gracie was staring at me. Expecting me to fix things. It was the stare the artist had captured in the sketch.

The sketch! I had an idea. Quietly I withdrew into the stairwell. I shut the door.

Removing the rolled-up sketch from my backpack, I put it inside the new tube. Now the tube felt about the same weight as the dented one.

I opened the door again.

Sherry was checking her diamond-studded watch.

"Soon I'll call a cab," she informed Smythe. "Would you carry our trunk down?"

Smythe looked unhappily at the four-foot-high, five-foot-wide trunk. "It's kind of big for one person. Plus, I should get downstairs to let the next group in."

Sherry ignored him. She was busy patting her black hair with her flashy-ringed hands. "I'll carry the mailing tube."

She swiveled to face the trunk.

Chapter Eleven

Gracie screamed.

Her aunt knelt beside her. "What is it, sweetie?" Her voice held a note of impatience. Sherry was not the maternal type.

"The bridge—someone's jumping off!" Gracie ran to the window.

Sherry followed. She, Gracie and Smythe all stared out.

"Over there!" Gracie exclaimed.

I tiptoed to the trunk. I placed on top the new, unbent tube containing the sketch. I tiptoed back into the stairwell and pulled the door almost shut.

Smythe said, "That's just somebody looking at the scenery. Nobody's jumping."

Sherry shrugged. "My niece is imaginative."

She stepped to the trunk. She picked up the tube. She shook it, and she smiled.

I shut the door. Holding the dented tube, I hurried down the stairs. I could hear the poster moving inside the tube, *ssshhh-ah, ssshhh-ah*, like a castanet.

I thought of Gracie opening her tube when she got home. Instead of the scary Death Drop poster, she'd find the sketch of her and me. A way nicer souvenir.

I passed another door. Then I heard footsteps above and behind me. And every few seconds a *thunk!*

It was Smythe, lugging that heavy trunk down the stairs. And the trunk crashing into the wall every few seconds.

The *thunk*s grew louder. He was getting closer.

My ribs were too sore to run down the rest of the stairs. I went back to the door I'd just passed. I opened it, stepped through.

I was behind a screen. Sherry's welcome video was playing on the other side of it.

Somebody called, "Hey! Who's behind the screen?"

I was casting a shadow. I hurried around the screen and mixed in with the crowd.

I changed my plan. I didn't want Smythe to spot me at the entrance. I'd follow everyone to the top. I'd ride down the Death Drop with them. Then I'd exit through the gift shop.

That made sense. Go with the flow.

The crowd shuffled around the corner to the portrait. I paused with them. Persephone had put her spell on me. I wanted to see her sad face, her haunting blue eyes.

I looked at the portrait.

And—

No spell.

I squinted. Persephone had the same beautiful face. The same thick dark hair, satiny dress, pomegranate in her hand.

The difference was, I couldn't feel her sadness. The first time I'd seen the portrait, she'd sent her feelings right out to me.

Maybe the first impression was always the strong one. Maybe after that the portrait lost its power.

Dieter had felt the same. *Seeing it a second time was kind of a letdown.*

I trudged around the next corner. I thought of the painter, Dante Rossetti. Obsessed with his model, he'd painted portrait after portrait of her. He'd put everything he had into them. The effort had ended up killing him—but not before he'd created a whole series of real, living Persephones on canvas.

At least, she'd seemed real the first time I saw the portrait. As opposed to the second time, when she looked beautiful but boring. Not lifelike at all.

My steps slowed. Not lifelike was how Persephone looked in the portrait in the elevator. Correction. In the *copy* of the portrait.

I stopped. In my mind I placed the portrait in the elevator beside the portrait I'd just seen. The two weren't that different.

In fact, they weren't different at all.

Which might mean—

The portrait on display wasn't the original.

Images flashed through my brain. The old woman fainting. Smythe, then the guard, rushing to the scene. The rest of the visitors gawking.

For those moments, the portrait had been left alone. Someone could have removed it and left a copy in its place.

I had to be sure. I needed to examine the portrait up close. If I still thought it was a fake, I'd let the cops know.

They might just laugh. Me, a kid. A baseball pitcher. What did I know?

But Dieter would back me up. On second view, he'd found the portrait a letdown. And he was a brainiac, a scholar.

The cops couldn't ignore both of us. They'd have to check into it.

I needed to wait until closing time, when no one was around. Till then, I knew just the place to hide.

The last of this group was moving around the next turn. I went back down the passageway. I reached the plastic trees with fake pomegranates. I hid behind a tree trunk.

I heard Smythe's voice in the passage behind the trees.

"Great acting job you did today."

In response, a shrill laugh rang out.

Then a frail, quaking voice—the voice of the white-haired old lady who'd fainted. "I should be on the stage. I fooled 'em all!"

The old lady's words puzzled me. And what was she doing here? She'd left by taxi. The sales clerk had seen her go.

The fake pomegranates shook. Smythe and the old woman were pushing through to the main passageway. Smythe's hand almost hit me in the face.

He didn't see me. But I saw him— and the old lady.

It wasn't an old lady though.

It was Sherry Moore.

Chapter Twelve

Sherry was the fainter.

It had been an act. A convincing one. I'd believed it. So had the guard. So had everyone else.

But Smythe hadn't been there. He'd left, on the pretext of finding a cab for the sick old lady. Who wasn't sick or old.

Smythe had gone to the portrait. With no one around, he had removed it. Hung a copy in its place.

That's what he'd started to remind Sherry. *I was the one who...*

Before Sherry sharply cut him off.

Why steal the portrait?

I didn't have to be a brainiac to figure that out. Sherry was in financial trouble. She would sell the portrait. For a Rossetti, some black-market art dealer would pay a huge amount of money.

Posing as the sick old lady, Sherry had taken off in a taxi. The girl in the souvenir shop had seen her.

Not her face though. Faking coughs, Sherry had kept a handkerchief over her features. Just in case.

Off-site, Sherry had doffed the wig. She'd restored her usual thick makeup and put on her flashy jewelry. She'd returned in a limo. That explained

Smythe's panic about the dad with the video camera. He didn't want anyone guessing at the old lady–Sherry switch.

One thing didn't fit. Why bring Gracie to Vancouver? Why have a loud-mouthed kid around? Loudmouths caused trouble.

And Gracie *had* caused trouble. Me.

So why bring her here in the first place?

Smythe and Sherry were walking ahead of me. I followed them partway around the next turn. They would be by the painting now.

I listened in.

Sherry was telling the guard, "You're done for the day. You can go. Smythe will lock up."

Whistling, the guard went behind the portrait to the employee passage and stairs.

When the sound of his whistling faded, Sherry marched up to the portrait. She studied it.

She said, "It won't be long before someone figures out this is a fake. You know what to do?"

Smythe nodded. "I blame it on the guard. I say I saw him switching the fake portrait for the real one."

Sherry's back was to Smythe. I saw Sherry break into her mean *gotcha!* smile.

I didn't think that tough guard was going to take the blame so easily. Sherry didn't think so either.

Sherry and the guard would blame Smythe. After all, Smythe had been the one alone with the real portrait. The guard had been helping a sick old lady. Sherry had been off-site—or so she would claim.

Smythe's fingerprints were probably all over the fake portrait. He was going to take the rap, and big-time.

I wondered how Smythe could be such a sap. I guessed greed had gotten the better of him. He was seeing dollar signs when he should have been seeing danger signs.

Then I realized it wasn't just greed. As he watched Sherry, Smythe's face got the same expression I'd seen outside— sucky and adoring.

He had a crush on her. A killer crush. He was going to self-destruct over a crush.

Like Dante Rossetti.

The painting must still be in the tower. Smythe couldn't have staggered out to the busy sidewalk with it. Even wrapped up, a package that big would attract attention.

If I could find the portrait, I would carry it out. And I would *want* attention. I would yell at the top of my lungs for everyone to look.

I tried to think what hiding place Smythe would choose. The office by the entrance? Too chancy. Someone might walk in.

The room where I'd found Gracie? No. I would have seen it.

Sherry said, "This is where I bid you farewell, Smythe. Gracie is waiting for me in the office. Our cab is coming."

"Yes, ma'am." Smythe shuffled his feet. He looked unhappy.

"I meet my buyer in London in a week. He'll pay me for *Persephone*, then smuggle her off to his oh-so-secluded estate. I will send your cut."

Smythe started to speak. He choked, cleared his throat. "W-will I ever see you again?"

"Safer not to," Sherry said briskly. "Now, Smythe. Make sure no one is around when you leave. We don't want any witnesses when you spirit our little package out of Death Drop."

Spirit out that huge portrait? Lug, heave or portage, even. But *spirit out*?

Sherry wouldn't want to risk taking the painting on the plane. Security might want to examine a package of that size. The plan must be for Smythe to mail or FedEx the portrait to her.

I couldn't think about that now. I had to concentrate. Where had Smythe hidden the portrait?

Smythe and Sherry started down the passage toward me. I ran ahead and ducked into the fake pomegranates.

As they passed, Smythe checked the time on his cell phone. "Ten to six," he commented. "Almost closing."

At the top of the tower, the last lineup would be waiting for the elevator. The people would be fidgeting. They would be excited and nervous about the big drop.

While they waited, they'd gawk at the scene beside them. Persephone at cliff's edge. The eerie, glowing pomegranate in her hand.

There was also the fake forest, but nobody would look at that. They'd fix their gaze on—

I drew in my breath so fast I almost inhaled one of the pomegranates. *Everyone would fix their gaze on Persephone.*

The fake forest, with its plastic trees and bushes, was the ideal place to stash the portrait!

I was willing to bet that's where Smythe had hidden it.

Once the last passengers had stepped into the elevator, Smythe would retrieve the portrait and smuggle it out.

I had to get there first.

Chapter Thirteen

I pushed through the pomegranates to the employee passage. I ran up the twisting stairs. I felt the metal tube bouncing in my backpack.

I reached the top of the stairs and another round door. I gripped the handle. I paused. I knew I was at the top of the tower. But I didn't know where the door came out. It might open right in the elevator guy's face.

I could already hear Edwin's long, gusty sigh. *You again.*

I pushed the door open slowly.

I was at the base of the cliff. In front of me was the circle of black jets. A neon red line ran around the outside of them.

A sign in front of the red line read, *WARNING! STAY OUTSIDE THE CIRCLE. IF FLAMES CATCH ON ANYTHING, FIRE COULD SPREAD.*

Past the circle of jets, in a corner, were piled the spare fake boulders I'd noticed before.

Above me, the cliff's edge jutted way out. I knew the Persephone mannequin with the glowing pomegranate was on it.

The door fell shut behind me. All at once I felt claustrophobic. I wanted to keep the door open.

I turned, twisted the handle.

It wouldn't budge.

I remembered the panicky scream I'd heard. *You idiots! Listen to me—this is not part of the show!* I'd been right. The scream wasn't a special effect. It was Smythe. He'd been here. The door had stuck for him too—when the flames were soaring.

The flames stayed inside the red circle. He would have been safe. Still, I couldn't blame him for freaking out. But why had he been down here in the first place?

Maybe I'd been wrong. Maybe he hadn't stashed the portrait on the cliff, among the fake trees.

Maybe he'd hidden it here.

I squinted through the dimness. Could the portrait fit between those fake boulders?

I walked past the circle of jets and the red line around them. Above, I heard

Edwin warning people about the elevator's forty-miles-per-hour drop.

I reached the boulders. I shone my cell-phone light.

One of the boulders wasn't round.

It was large, rectangular and covered with a black garbage bag.

The portrait!

Time to spring you, Persephone. I tore the garbage bag away.

But there was no Persephone inside. Only the frame.

The portrait had been removed.

Smythe had hidden Persephone somewhere else. She wasn't down here.

I headed for the door. I remembered the creak and thud I'd heard after Smythe's scream. Smythe had managed to wrestle the door open. I'd have to do the same.

My eyes were getting used to the dimness. I noticed something I hadn't before. At one side, by the wall, a long ladder leaned against the cliff.

Smythe couldn't have escaped by the ladder. People in the lineup would have seen him emerge on the cliff.

But I didn't care about being seen. I didn't have to bother forcing the door open. I could climb out of here.

I was halfway up the ladder when the flames burst upward.

I'd been expecting them, so I wasn't surprised. I wasn't scared either. I didn't panic like Smythe had.

On the wall beside me a video appeared. It showed the huge, red, reaching hands I'd seen before. From the lineup, it had seemed the hands were right in the flames.

Yet another thing in this tower that seemed to be happening but wasn't.

I reached the cliff. I stepped off the ladder—then stumbled over the edge of a carpet. No, not a carpet. Fake grass. I lurched forward.

In the lineup, a woman screamed.

I realized what I must look like from a distance—a Frankenstein-monster figure charging out of the flames.

"Oh, come on, Ellen," snapped the woman's friend. "Quit stalling." She shoved Ellen into the elevator.

Edwin looked around to see what had scared the woman. He spotted me.

I waved.

"No!" he shouted. He held up his hands to block his view of me. "I'm not seeing you. *You're not here.*"

He pushed onto the elevator with the last people in line. "This dude is clocking out," he announced.

The doors closed. The elevator jolted, hung for a moment. The first scare. The false alarm. There were screams, then nervous laughter.

The elevator plunged. The screams— louder, longer, more terrified—echoed back up to me.

I pushed through the fake trees. I overturned fake bushes. *Where was the portrait?*

"Looking for something?"

I whipped around. It was Smythe.

His eyes glittered. He was carrying an ax.

Chapter Fourteen

It was like something out of a cheesy horror flick. I laughed. "Seriously, Smythe? You're coming after me with an *ax*?"

Smythe licked his teeth. "Get out of here. Now."

"On one condition. You get out with me. You can't trust the manager. I know you have a thing for her, but think about it. She'll blame you for stealing the painting."

Smythe flushed.

I added, "I highly doubt she's going to send you your cut. Why would she bother, when you're the fall guy?"

Smythe reddened. I'd gotten to him, to his self-doubts. He wasn't the most confident guy. That's what Sherry had played on. She'd flattered him, made him first her assistant, then her partner in crime.

I put on what I hoped was a friendly smile. Maybe I could win him over. Get him to talk.

And, with my voice-memo app, record what he said.

I felt for my phone.

Then I remembered. I'd given the phone to Dieter. Where *was* Dieter anyway? He was supposed to meet Coach at six.

Smythe was white-knuckling the ax. Okay, so my charm offensive hadn't worked. On to plan B. Leave Death Drop. Contact the police—and watch for Smythe to exit. He'd have the portrait with him.

I held out my hands in a gesture of surrender. "You win. I've bothered you enough. So…now I'll just quietly go."

I started away.

Smythe followed me. "I want to know what you know."

"Nothing," I assured him. "Think of my brain as a large, empty parking lot."

He was still holding the ax.

I reached for the end of the metal mailing tube sticking out of my backpack. I whipped the tube out, brandished it at Smythe. "*En garde!*"

He scowled. "That's Death Drop property."

"Technically, this is the property of Gracie Moore," I told him. "It's the souvenir Sherry picked out for her. The poster of people crashing into flames. Nice, huh?"

Smythe froze. He went even paler than usual. A mummy hue.

He also dropped the ax. It landed blade first in a plastic log, where it stuck.

I stared at the ax. Then I understood. Smythe hadn't brought the ax to use on me. He'd planned to chop up the frame. Carrying out the frame might attract attention. In pieces, it wouldn't. It would be the "little package" Sherry had talked about.

I turned away. I started down the cliff.

But Smythe pounded up behind. He gave me a violent shove.

I went sprawling forward. The whole cliff shook. I scrambled up, ready to belt Smythe.

Then I saw Persephone wobbling. With the cliff's edge curving out over the flames, the mannequin would fall right into them.

I remembered the sign: *IF FLAMES CATCH ON ANYTHING, FIRE COULD SPREAD.*

I had to stop Persephone from going over.

I dropped the metal tube. I slid my backpack off. I shot past Smythe.

The mannequin was tipping. I made a running dive for it. When I hit the ground, pain flashed through my injured ribs.

I grabbed the falling mannequin by an ankle. I stopped its fall.

I sat up, wincing.

Smythe was coming toward me. His hands were clawlike. They reached out.

But not for me.

It was the tube he grabbed.

I was holding my ribs. I couldn't move or speak. It hurt even to breathe. I could only watch him, bewildered.

Why did he care about a metal tube containing a poster?

He shot me a look of triumph. He saw I was sidelined, couldn't stop him.

He started down the cliff. The tube gleamed in his hands.

The tube…

My mind rewound to Sherry, picking up the tube I'd left on the trunk. The tube replacing the one I'd dented. The tube I'd put the sketch inside.

Sherry had shaken the tube. Smiled with satisfaction at the sound she heard inside. Insisted on carrying the tube out of the tower.

Because it wasn't a poster she thought was in the tube.

It was Rossetti's painting.

After removing the portrait from its frame, Smythe had rolled it up. He'd put it in a metal mailing tube. He'd given the tube to Sherry—who presented it to Gracie as a souvenir poster.

That's why Sherry had brought Gracie to Vancouver. To carry the tube back to London. Nobody would think twice about a kid with a souvenir. Customs officials were on the lookout for terrorists, not little girls with posters.

When I'd started asking about Gracie, Smythe had pretended not to know anything about her. He and Sherry didn't want attention drawn to a kid who would soon be carting around a stolen masterpiece.

Except things hadn't gone according to plan. Gracie wasn't carting around the portrait. I was—till just now.

As soon as I'd said the tube was Gracie's, Smythe realized there'd been a switch. He knew this tube contained the painting. That's why he'd gone such a ghoulish shade of pale.

I had to get the tube back from Smythe.

I staggered up. Pain tore at my ribs.

Smythe reached the bottom of the hill. He jumped over the chain separating the cliff scene from the lineup area. He started down the passageway.

Then we heard noises. Yelling, footsteps pounding.

Coach and Dieter ran around the bend. Smythe gaped at them. Swiveling, he sprinted for the elevator. He punched the button. He was going to take the express route down.

I grabbed my backpack, felt inside for my baseball. I couldn't chase after Smythe. Not in this much pain. I couldn't yell out an explanation to Coach and Dieter. That would take too much time.

But I could throw.

Chapter Fifteen

The elevator arrived. The doors opened. Smythe jumped in. He turned around, face half fearful, half smug.

I raised my baseball for the pitch of my life. I threw.

Smythe started to raise his free hand. Maybe he thought he could catch the ball. But it was my best shot. It was an air-crusher. It beat time. It stopped for nobody.

The ball whipped into the elevator. It knocked the tube out of Smythe's hands.

The tube flew up, a long, whirling baton. The doors clamped shut on one end of it.

With the tube in their grip, the doors couldn't close. The elevator stayed put.

Struck you out, Smythe.

But Smythe wasn't giving up. He pulled at the tube. It began disappearing between the doors.

"Stop him!" I yelled. "*He's got the painting!*"

Coach shot me a *whaaaat?* look. But, mad at me or not, he ran.

Dieter ran faster. Death Drop may have been faster than gravity, but this guy was faster than light. For those few seconds, I could swear he was more blur than flesh.

Dieter reached the elevator. He gripped the end of the tube. Smythe was stronger—but the Deet slowed him down.

Coach joined him. He grabbed the tube too. I limped up to them. With three of us on one end of the tug-of-war, we got it out easily.

Nothing was keeping the doors open now. They shut.

The elevator gave its false-alarm jolt. It paused. Then it crashed downward. We heard the cartoony Persephone's scream—followed by an agonized, real-life scream.

I realized why. Smythe had been busy trying to wrestle the tube back into the elevator. He hadn't thought to belt himself in. Now it was too late.

"Yowzers," I said under my breath. The image of Smythe being tossed around like a vegetable inside a blender wasn't pretty.

Soon, from a distance, we heard a different type of screaming. Police sirens, summoned by the 9-1-1 call Coach had made.

From the tube, Coach pulled out the canvas Dante Rossetti had painted almost a century and a half ago. He unrolled it.

For once the Deet didn't say a word. The three of us gazed at the sad-faced woman, whose only mistake had been eating a few pomegranate seeds.

Persephone's blue eyes shone out at me. And reminded me of a girl with green eyes.

A girl with a notepad. Except it hadn't been a notepad. *I wasn't taking notes, pitcher boy.*

I started back down the passage.

Coach called, "I bet you get a medal for finding this portrait. And Zeke?" He gave me a thumbs-up. "Stellar shot, buddy."

"See you at practice," I called back.

My gaze went to Dieter. I thought of how fast he'd run. Coach wasn't a coach for nothing. He'd have noticed it too.

I grinned. "See you *both* at practice."

She was sitting in a canvas chair on the sidewalk. A man was buying a seagull sketch from her.

I waited till the man left. Then I approached.

"Hey."

She brightened. Her eyes were just as green as I remembered. "Hey, pitcher boy."

"Sell many Death Drop posters today?" I asked.

Her smile faded. "A few. But now it seems I'm out of business. Smythe just hobbled by. One foot seemed to be sprained, and he was cradling his left shoulder. Between moans of pain he told me that Death Drop was closing. That I'm out of a job."

I knelt beside her. "You'll get to draw more. That's a good thing. And maybe you'll have time to come to a baseball game."

That got her smiling again, kind of shyly. "Could be, pitcher boy. Anyhow, I won't mind being free of Sherry. She was a miserable boss. And Smythe! Whine, whine, whine."

I glanced around. "Where'd Smythe go?"

"He waved for a cab and limped into it. He kept glancing back like somebody was after him."

The sirens wailed closer. I said, "I think a whole bunch of somebodies will be after him, very soon."

I picked up another sketch. I studied the airplane signature. "I'm Zeke. And let me guess. Your name is 747."

She laughed. "It's Jett. And I'm betting you're the one who bought my sketch of the little girl reaming you out."

I nodded. "You nailed us. Gracie, stubborn and scared. Me, not wanting to be bothered with her."

"You did bother with her though," said Jett. "I could see that. I could see you were going to take care of her. That's why I had to draw you two."

I remembered something. "In the gift shop, you started to tell me something. My buddy Dieter interrupted."

Jett nodded. "You asked me if I'd seen a lost blond kid. I said no. Then I wondered if you meant the little girl who'd been yelling at you. Did everything turn out okay? That's what I wanted to ask."

A police car screamed to the curb, lights blazing. Two officers barged out. They hurried to the Death Drop. Jumping over the turnstile, they ran inside.

"The kid's safe," I assured Jett. "On her way to London. To her parents."

Jett looked wistful. "I'd love to go to London. All those art galleries."

I thought of Sherry and Gracie arriving in London. Of Sherry greedily seizing the kid's mailing tube.

I pictured Sherry opening the tube. Dollar signs would be dancing in her eyes.

She'd slide out the artwork, only to see—

"Imagine showing your work in London," Jett was saying.

I grinned. "That may happen a lot sooner than you think."

Acknowledgments

I would like to express my gratitude to editor Melanie Jeffs for all her guidance over the years. Hugs and best wishes for your new adventures to come!

Death Drop is Melanie Jackson's fifth mystery in the Orca Currents. Her other titles, *The Big Dip, Fast Slide, High Wire* and *Eye Sore*, all feature thrilling forms of amusement. Melanie lives in Vancouver, British Columbia. Visit www.melaniejacksonblog.wordpress.com.

Titles in the Series

orca currents